THE 5 PILLARS
OF BUILDING A SUCCESSFUL PRACTICE

DR. DANIEL KALISH

THE 5 PILLARS
OF BUILDING A SUCCESSFUL PRACTICE

DR. DANIEL KALISH

THE KALISH INSTITUTE

TABLE OF CONTENTS

INTRODUCTION

Those of us in private practice all want to relieve human suffering and change people's lives. This is why we signed up to be healthcare practitioners in the first place. Achieving those goals requires a blend of three key things: **clinical skills, people skills, and business skills**.

Occasionally I meet a superb clinician who is naturally gifted with all three—someone who has mastered patient treatment, has well-honed patient communication skills, and is adept at managing a business. The rest of us need to learn these components of running a successful functional medicine practice through purposeful study and focus.

I call these key elements the three P's: **practitioners**, **patients**, and **practices**. When brought together in just the right way, they result in outstanding clinical results and financial success. If there is one weak link in the chain, the entire endeavor falters. Lack of a clear clinical model, underdeveloped communication and sales skills, and poor business management plague our profession and limit even the best-intentioned practitioners.

I had to learn each of the three P's separately from different people, none of whom had the big picture in mind. The doctors who taught me my clinical skills weren't very good at business, my communications teachers had no clue about clinical models, and those who taught me my business management skills weren't even in the healthcare field! What a mess. Those of us striking out on our own to create small, integrative private practices need to focus equally on all three areas to make it in the long term.

My specific route to mastery of the three P's was random and unplanned. Initially, I thought I just needed to learn the clinical side. Most of my first five years of training was taken up by understanding the practice of functional medicine, including the science, protocols, theory, and application. Then after a few years of running a busy practice, I realized that many of my patients, though they liked me, had no idea what I was talking about and no sense of a bigger picture other than that I could help them. At this stage, I began to study communication skills: How can we get our message across? Is it what we say, how we say it, body language, showing a diagram, choosing our vocabulary carefully? And, importantly, what do we want to communicate? How do we convince someone to spend $1500 on lab testing that their insurance won't cover? How do we persuade someone to stop eating gluten?

> Around my seventh year in practice, I realized that sales wasn't a **small** part of what I did

Much of what we do in the treatment room involves convincing people to make challenging changes in their lives. While studying communication, I realized that much of what I was doing was actually "selling." Sales always felt wrong, and it seemed to be somewhat tawdry and beneath me. I was doctoring, not selling. Then one day I woke up to the reality that I was learning how to "sell" health. I had to sell lab kits and supplement programs that would help people lose weight. I had to sell exercise programs and sell diet programs that eliminated depression and fatigue. Around my seventh year in practice, I realized that sales wasn't a **small** part of what I did; instead, sales encompassed the most important part of what I did. Those who bought the lab kits and supplements, and bought into the diet, exercise, and meditation programs all became healthier, while those who didn't would never see the improvement they wanted.

After ten years of clinical training and four years of learning how to communicate and how to sell, I realized I was running a small business. Honestly, if you had asked me in my fifth year of practice if I was running a small business, I would have denied it. I was so engrossed in taking care of patients and so deep in continuing my study of biochemistry and nutrition that I didn't realize my staff were not friends (they were employees) and that my income was really the P on my P & L. I didn't know what my margins were; I just knew that most every month I covered all the bills and could usually fund my retirement plan. My business plan was "cover the credit cards next month and pay rent."

Fortunately, after I learned from the best functional medicine teachers, I was exposed to business concepts from a variety of business leaders, financial consultants, investors, and entrepreneurs in other industries. These businesspeople helped me create several financially successfully clinics. I, myself, went through three distinct phases in building my practice, each taking many years to complete.

At the Kalish Institute, we strive to shorten the learning curve and provide our students with a one-stop-shopping approach. We have a clear, successful clinical model that has been in use for decades. We have scripts and lessons on how to further your patient communication skills. And we have a business-oriented focus that combines the three key elements of practitioners, patients, and practices so you can create a profitable business that does not lead to practitioner burnout.

My primary professional interest, outside my own private practice, is to help fellow practitioners create profitable, independent, and sustainable practices. I want to reach those looking for a mentorship and coaching model by teaching you what I was taught by my mentors.

1

THE THREE P's AND THE BUSINESS OF HEALTH OF PRACTITIONERS

MY THESIS

Building a successful functional medicine practice relies on three key factors, what I call the three P's: practitioners, patients, and practices.

Practitioners includes you, your staff, and all the people involved in the delivery of your services and treatment model.

Patients includes those you care for and the communication used to deliver quality patient care.

Practice encompasses all the logistics and business systems required to keep your clinic running well.

An equal emphasis on practitioners, patients, and practices creates a healthy and supportive work environment for you, one in which your health matters and you do not need to make sacrifices. In fact, in a well-executed example of this model, your health comes first, your knowledge is very well rewarded financially, and, at the same time, patients get incredible results.

PRACTITIONERS AND PRACTICES

Over a sixteen-year period of teaching functional medicine, I've taken about one thousand practitioners through my training programs. I've connected in person with most of them. I know their individual stories and the states of their practices, and I've come to understand what they are looking for both professionally and personally. One not so surprising finding is how stressed out we all were in school! As well, most of us were under a lot of pressure when we started our practices. And so it goes. It is remarkable how burned out and unhealthy most of us become after grinding away for a decade or more in practice. Few of us know enough to pull ourselves out of the downward spiral of practitioner burnout. Many of us love our work but face a high-stress work environment without being robust and at peak health ourselves. We are usually working too many hours mired in a practice that is not as emotionally or financially rewarding as it could be.

Physician burnout has three well-known characteristics: exhaustion, cynicism, and doubt. The first step in the Kalish Method training program is to test and treat ourselves. It is difficult to create a vital, fun, life-fulfilling practice when you are just getting by.

The Three Symptoms

1. Exhaustion: You are tired on an energetic, emotional, and spiritual level.

2. Cynicism: You have lost your ability to care, empathize, and connect with your patients, staff, and co-workers.

3. Doubt: You may begin to doubt that your work really makes a difference or question the quality of the care you provide.

To combat practitioner burnout, we give every new student in the Kalish mentorship a free adrenal stress test to determine their level of burnout and begin to remedy the situation. It's "physician, heal thyself" for real, not just in words but in deeds. If your cortisol and DHEA levels are normal on your initial adrenal stress test, then a very big congratulations to you. You can join the other three practitioners who are in this category. If not, we can get to work sorting through your health issues as a learning tool for the materials you will present to your patients.

BUILDING A FOUNDATION

A big part of being successful in practice is being successful in business. When starting to focus on business issues, the first thing to consider is your unique niche. What can you be the best at? For my practice, it was always female hormone programs. Others may choose autism, autoimmune disease, athletes, new moms, infertility, chronic fatigue, fibromyalgia, diabetes, eating disorders, alcohol recovery, peak performance, ADHD, pediatrics, or geriatrics. It doesn't really matter, as there are more than enough patients in any category you may choose. What does matter is that you excel at treating the patients in your niche—that you are a master.

Once you have your unique niche settled, it needs to be profitable. So often we see practices that are quite successful from a clinical standpoint (i.e., the patients are getting well), but the clinic isn't profitable. I'm not talking about any of us becoming rich, but I am expecting that we can work reasonable hours that allow for daily meditation, exercise, and preparing healthy meals as well as plenty of time with family and friends and some downtime for ourselves to reflect and grow as individual healers. You can't work eighty hours a week and further your growth as a healer on the side. To ensure a goal of profitability is within reach based on the amount of hours you want to dedicate to your practice, early on it will be important to create a business plan and map out an estimated number of patients and lab and supplement sales as well as expenses required to run your practice.

Once you've found a niche and you're sure it's economically feasible, then it comes down to passion. Is this something that's just a job to you, or is it truly what you want for yourself? Will it be fulfilling? Will you be happy to have *Dr. So-and-so focused on X* on your tombstone for everyone to see for all eternity? I'm passionate about functional medicine and always have been. Now I'm passionate about teaching. There aren't a lot of functional medicine teachers, so it's a good niche and it pays well. The Kalish Method mentorship allows me to do something that I'm passionate about, that I'm very good at, and that I'm able to make good money doing. Oftentimes my days full of classes and teaching are more emotionally meaningful for me than my days off.

Recently I spoke with a doctor who wanted to start a functional-medicine-based practice working exclusively with children. She was passionate about working with children with autism, having come from a conventional medical setting working with children, but she had no experience in functional medicine. We agreed that it probably wasn't economically feasible to work with such a challenging patient population while learning the basics of functional medicine and agreed that she could have a general pediatric practice and in two or three years move into working with more difficult cases.

I met another physician, Jeff, who had over forty years of medical practice under his belt. He had a full practice, a great niche combining acupuncture with his MD degree, and had all the passion in the world but wasn't making much money. He was spending several hours with new patients and not billing fully for his time. He would discount supplements, give away services, and in general acted as a "healer" rather than a "businessman." Coming near to retirement, Jeff was ready to punch up the 401K He used the Kalish Method mentorship program to streamline his practice and build an economic engine in it, demonstrating that physicians can be a healer and make a wage commensurate with the professional degrees they have.

Another example, Ed, is a very successful chiropractor in New York City. Just this past year, he decided to follow what he is truly best at doing. Although a highly skilled clinician, he is even better at marketing and sales. Now he has an associate in his practice and is happily doing sales and marketing talks and directing new patients into his clinic for his associate to treat.

I find a lot of this has to do with age. I'm fifty years old now, and doctors my age want different things than those in their thirties. Older doctors are okay with slowing down and not having to do everything for everyone every day. We want vacations, retirement accounts, time alone, and time with our partners and kids. We are okay with bringing in the next generation of practitioners and getting them trained and in action. We aren't interested in building a huge dream clinic but more often are ready to scale back and be streamlined and efficient. Take some time to think about where you are in your career and what is most important to you.

CHAPTER

2

MY STORY

When I was twenty-two, my father, Richard Kalish, died. He was only fifty-eight years old. His father, Max Kalish, had died at age fifty-two, and I took on the belief that I was in danger of dying young myself. This fear drove my behavior for many years and motivated me to study integrative medicine, having seen previous generations of Kalish men die young while solely relying on conventional medical treatments. Eventually I stumbled across functional medicine and the concept of finding the underlying problems of health issues. I was hooked. With this, I believed I would have the opportunity to live a long, healthy life.

THE IMPORTANCE OF MENTORS

Fortunately, I met a series of mentors early on. They were willing to train me, seeing the potential in a young and eager practitioner. John R. Lee, MD was the first, and while I was still in my first year as an intern in the chiropractic college clinic, Dr. Lee would consult with me on each and every new patient. In my second year, I met Glenn Frieder, ND, DC, who spent over four years teaching me fundamental naturopathic concepts and introduced me to the vast subject of clinical nutrition. Finally, a short time after graduating, Bill Timmins, ND appeared, and my training accelerated. The Kalish Method is a reflection of the lessons from these practitioners and many more who remain unmentioned.

Dr. Timmins taught me the critical component of lab-based functional medicine assessments combined with lifestyle changes. Year after year, he drilled into me the need to test the patient thoroughly in three key areas prior to initiating treatments. Neuroendocrine, gut, and detox—over and over. I can still remember him saying, "The key to effective treatment programs is the quality of the diagnostic data available prior to setting up the treatment program." He must have told me that a hundred times.

He was a teacher, an educator, and also a highly skilled clinician. A very animated and loving person, he focused on chronically ill patients who were quite sick. He devoted himself to that demographic because he had experienced his own chronic health crisis. Yet despite his focus on working with the chronically ill, he always did the basics first, something I have very much embodied in the Kalish Method.

My personal involvement with Dr. Timmins started because of a woman named Carolyn. She was a new patient to whom I wanted to prescribe progesterone cream. She said she'd only use it if we did some testing to show she needed it (smart lady), so I ran pre and post labs on her, and her progesterone levels went from undetectable to over 5,000 (i.e., ten times normal) in just five days of using the progesterone cream. This, needless to say, freaked me out since I'd been using progesterone cream with hundreds of patients without ever doing lab work, assuming it was all going to work out fine because their symptoms were improving.

This brings me to one of my favorite Dr. Timmins phrases, "Do the test or die like the rest." (In fact, some of the guys working at his lab had these words put on a T-shirt and walked around the office with the slogan emblazoned on their chests in large letters.) My initial coaching call with Dr. Timmins, to discuss Carolyn, led to literally years of conversations on every imaginable functional medicine topic. We met several times a week for many years of personal mentorship. We reviewed every new patient and every lab test and had long conversations on the theory and application of functional medicine. He taught me one test, one body system at a time—first female hormones, then adrenals and thyroid, and then a year or so later GI workups. When he felt I was ready, after a few years of study, we covered detox.

DEVELOPING A SYSTEM

After about six years working side by side with Dr. Timmins, I had all the basic information I needed and my training as an apprentice to my generous mentors was complete. They had passed the torch of clinical knowledge on to me. The system I now teach stems from these early years and is an organized and simplified reflection of the basic work I was taught.

Over the years, I've received many pearls of wisdom from these teachers, but if I could put my thumb on the main principle I have taken away—the ideas I still think of each week in practice today—it would be the idea of treatment flow.

Dr. Timmins would say, **"Most practitioners are using the 'Ready, Fire, Aim' approach."** In other words, it's easy to treat first before you know exactly what's going on.

Dr. Curtis Buddhing, another of my mentors, explained that "people pay us for what we know and not what we do." This means that just understanding why someone becomes sick, even though you haven't done anything yet to correct his or her issues, has significant value. For example, I've reversed several autoimmune cases and a few cases of Crohn's disease just with diet changes. I was being paid for my ability to identify the root cause of those patients' problems.

Dr. Timmins also said, "The better you become as a practitioner, the fewer supplements you will use and the shorter your programs will be."

This translates to how we as healers do not need to rely solely on "treatments" from the outside and that it's not the volume of products or labs we use but the specifics of knowing the key levers to move to get the patient better. Sometimes cutting out caffeine impacts a person more than all the adrenal supplements one could prescribe, and sometimes one key supplement will take care of three or four different symptoms.

And one of the most important things taught to me by Dr. Timmins that I've personally seen come true in my own practice is "80 percent of the success of functional medicine programs comes from bonding with the patients and getting them to implement the lifestyle changes." We use lab workups for diagnosing the underlying cause of symptoms, and we use lab workups to demonstrate the level of dysfunction present and to thereby motivate the patient to make lifestyle changes.

PRACTICE STRUGGLES AND ISSUES

After gaining clinical competence from four years of school and another five years in practice with several ongoing mentorships, I was ready for something new. Gone were the constant weekend seminars and reading up on the basics of nutritional supplements, treatments for common conditions, and figuring out what lab companies and supplement companies to use. My coaching time with Dr. Lee, Dr. Frieder, and Dr. Timmins had ground to a halt. Unknown to me, at that time my practice model was established.

What I did know was that I was tired of learning new things and wanted to focus on what I'd already learned and hone my skills. After nine straight years of continual study, I was ready to stop being a compulsive student always looking for the next shiny object, the next seminar, and that one super-special supplement. From a business perspective, the model was perfected. I was ready for growth and scaling.

Around this time, I realized I had worked my way into a chronic illness practice. When I first started to use the functional medicine tests and labs in my practice, I figured, as most docs do, that I'd perform the tests mainly on patients I was not helping already. This invariably meant the chronically ill patients who were unresponsive to my other forms of care. It made sense. However, this generated two problems. One, I was working with the hardest patient population with my new skills, and this made for a low percentage of positive results. Many patients were simply too sick to benefit greatly from this type of work. If you're in this situation and you throw your toughest cases at the lab work, it's likely that you too will be frustrated and feel like functional medicine doesn't work very well. You could get some patients better, but your cure rate would be low.

I didn't have a clue as to who were the best patients to do this work with. I persisted simply because I was determined to make this my life's work. Over time, as I became more and more proficient with lab workups and programs, my chronically ill patients typically started to get better, but it took several years to get my skills up to this point. I had developed a reputation as a practitioner who could treat the hardest cases, the patients who had been to a dozen doctors and no one had helped them. Soon my entire practice was chronically ill patients!

I then quickly burned out. I was working long hours, putting so much energy into each patient that I didn't have much left over for myself or my family. I wasn't making that much money either, given the number of hours I was working and the amount of stress I was under. Finally, when my son was born, I realized my practice's situation wasn't sustainable. I needed to create a different practice and business model—one that worked for me as well as it worked for my patients.

BREAKING THROUGH

I realized that functional medicine tests were originally developed for the most difficult patients—those I would call "chronically ill" who were unresponsive to traditional medical treatments and the typical alternative treatments—and that all of my teachers had that type of practice. Naturally I thought that was what I should do. I didn't even conceptualize that there was any other option.

Right at this time, something fortuitous occurred. I met new patient who was previously a patient of the famed osteopath Dr. Robert Fulford. Dr. Fulford was a legend, and I felt honored to meet someone who had been with the man for many years. I started to research Dr. Fulford more (he was featured in one of Dr. Andrew Weil's early books).

One thing Dr. Fulford did toward the end of his career was cap the age of the patients he would take on. He wanted to work only with people who were under the age of twenty-one because he saw the limits to his own life and that he would be able to impact only a fixed number of patients doing his hands-on healing work. He reasoned that getting an eighteen-year-old out of chronic pain would lead to more years of pain relief than getting a seventy-eight-year-old out of chronic pain.

Of course, this radical idea came to him only as he was advanced in age and had limited time to practice. This policy of his made me realize that there was some real value in my working with patients PRIOR to the onset of the more advanced health problems. If I could work with a healthier patient population, I could prevent many of the very conditions I'd gotten so adept at treating.

From this realization, I re-established my practice with an emphasis on early detection and prevention of chronic illness rather than exclusively treating the chronically ill. I quickly found the same tests and supplement programs could be modified for use with this healthier patient population. This was a huge breakthrough for me.

Actually, this reasonably healthy patient population was right in front of me. They were coming into my clinic every day for chiropractic adjustments. Then I thought that perhaps I could PREVENT chronic illness from developing by working with these patients at an earlier stage of declining health.

I began to direct my functional medicine programs to regular chiropractic patients by talking to them about what, besides their chiropractic problems, was going on with their health. Within two years, I'd transformed my practice to one with a few chronically ill patients and a lot of the walking wounded who were primed for this new (to me) model of functional medicine.

Now, fast forwarding to today, chronically ill patients make up approximately 10 to 15 percent of my practice and the majority of patients I work with have issues we can typically fix in six to twelve months' time. It's a win–win situation, benefiting both my patients and myself.

SOME LAST THOUGHTS

While I've chosen to move away from a chronic-illness-oriented practice, if you have the passion, time, energy, and emotional wherewithal for this type of practice, then I seriously applaud you. I just didn't have the personality for it. Our society needs all types of practitioners, and I encourage all doctors to create the type of practice they want for themselves. Just be clear what you want so you can create your practice and not wake up one morning wondering how you developed a practice that you'd never planned on.

3

THE THREE GROUPS
OF PRACTITIONERS

In my conversations with hundreds of doctors each year, I find three groups of practitioners out there: new practitioners; those transitioning from an existing practice in medicine, acupuncture, or chiropractic to a functional medicine module; and the veterans, or those with years of functional medicine experience who are looking to streamline their practice with a simple clinic model. Many of these doctors I meet are like I was in 1995, going to every available functional medicine seminar and knowledgeable on the subject but clueless as to how to build a profitable practice around a functional medicine framework. I'll address each of these groups individually in this chapter.

NEWCOMERS

The newcomers are usually still in school, returning from professional leave, or building from the ground up having just graduated. Financial and time pressures abound. The usual trajectory of spending years developing one's personalized practice model is daunting, almost over-whelming. In addition to not feeling clear what to do with each new patient, they face emotional insecurities about whether a given protocol will actually work (e.g., will this autoimmune patient really respond to a simple diet change?). The lack of clinical experience translates into not knowing what to expect in terms of patient outcomes. This in turn leads to a lack of confidence in charging out there and gathering new patients to help. Added to this uncertainty are the issues of generating income and establishing a consistent income stream.

I know with my first one hundred patients, I had absolutely no idea who would respond and what to tell people to expect. I proceeded with 100 percent blind faith and no certainty. Looking back, it's a miracle I kept moving forward. I owe all my current success to the mentors I met early on who had never spent a day in a classroom or as a faculty member but had successfully treated thousands of patients. My combination of classroom knowledge with mentorship from practicing physicians was what gave me all the opportunity in the world to succeed. I would still be eking by now if it weren't for the inspiration and training of practicing doctors stacked on top of my intellectual framework from seminars, books, and classes.

For those new to practice, the first five years after school require some concrete business decisions. You have to decide what kind of practice you want: **solo practice**, **group practice**, **or to become an associate**. A solo practice allows you to have the most independence; however, it is also the most risky choice and leaves you with the most individual pressures. A group practice in an integrative medicine clinic allows for the benefits of group synergy, but there are more logistical details and group politics to deal with. You will have a boss, colleagues, and a larger staff, all of which can be supportive or nerve wracking. Working as an associate allows you to avoid all the start-up costs and overhead expenses associated with opening a brand new clinic. But while it helps you avoid taking on even more financial debt, there is always a tendency for those in the associate position to become resentful over time and feel they could do a better job and make more money on their own.

One important concept to master early in your business planning is the idea of your "margin," or the percentage of overall revenue you collect and keep after all your costs are covered. So, if your practice generates $100,000 in a year, and your staff, rent, supplies, and all other expenses end up costing you $40,000, then your profit would be $60,000, giving you a 60 percent margin. That's a good margin. Anyone with a 60 percent margin in our industry is doing pretty well at keeping their overhead in line and managing their business. On the other hand, if your large integrative health clinic collects $1,000,000 a year, and your staff of seven, high rent, and other overhead costs add up to $800,000 a year, your profit is $200,000, leaving you with a 20 percent margin. Not so good.

I've run clinics at a 20 percent margin (large integrative clinics with lots of fancy equipment and a big staff) as well as solo practices with a 60 percent margin. The funny part is that $1,000,000 of revenue with a 20 percent margin gets you $200,000 at the end of the year, whereas a clinic revenue of $400,000 with a 60 percent margin provides you with $240,000 in profit. Ironically, oftentimes the smaller, lower-overhead clinic setting with less initial income can lead to more income for you at the end of the year—and (this is the most important point) with a lot less work. Before making any business decisions about what type of practice you want to embark upon, look at you potential total revenue, expenses, and margins. Be sure to factor in how many hours of your time will be required to run each of these various scenarios.

In my personal experience, the busiest time of my life was when I was running a large integrative health clinic with a staff of seven and a fifteen-hundred-square-foot space in a very high-rent area near the beach in Del Mar, California. We had a small gym, seven treatment rooms, back office and front office space, and offered services from functional medicine to acupuncture, to therapy and nutritional counseling, to exercise programs.

I worked nonstop, the clinic generated large amounts of cash, and with a 20 percent margin I ended up making around $14,000 per month ($168,000 per year). If you look at this based on the number of hours I worked, it was not a great deal. Let's do the math. $14,000 per month divided by 4.3 weeks in a month and an average work week of 50 hours is $14,000 divided by 4.3 divided by 50. That equals $65 an hour!

Later, after switching to a low-overhead, low-hours model, I collected $400,000 per year on a 60 percent margin, meaning I kept $240,000 per year of the $400,000 total collected. However, in this low-overhead model, I spent 10 hours a week with patients and 10 hours a week on administration, for a total of 20 hours a week of work. The math on that is $240,000 per year (or $20,000 month of profit) divided by 4.3 weeks and 20 hours a week of work, which put me at $232 an hour. That's a big pay raise from my large successful clinic years of making $65 an hour.

TRANSITIONING PRACTITIONERS

The second group of practitioners I speak with week in and week out are going through a transition. These experienced practitioners have an existing practice and want to change their model to functional medicine. They may be moving from an insurance-based practice to an all-cash practice. They may be moving from a conventional medicine setting as a psychiatrist, internist, or ob/gyn to an integrative setting, or from a chiropractic or acupuncture practice to something more focused on a lab-based functional medicine approach. Even NDs with extensive training in functional medicine may be looking to put a focused functional medicine component side by side with or in place of their existing practice.

In Silicon Valley, we have a saying that "selling to the install base" is your best way to increase revenue. What that means in plain English is, if you have existing customers, they are your best bet for building your business even if you are going in a new direction. Doctors with an existing practice have different concerns than those starting out. Some aspects of practice building will be much easier, and some will be much more challenging. Already having a patient base to build on helps tremendously with the start-up phase. However, old habits, dependency on insurance reimbursements, and staff that have a certain way of doing things can all add up to a level of inertia that one must overcome.

Within the transitioning practitioner group, I see two main types. The first type are those wanting to add functional medicine to their existing practice as a new service that they will offer alongside their existing treatments. For example, those who want to practice acupuncture half time and functional medicine half time or those who want to continue to do chiropractic adjustments two days a week and devote the rest of their time to functional medicine. The second type are interested in diving 100 percent into a functional medicine model, either selling their old practice or leaving that particular clinic to create something new and fresh that they have ownership and control over. I see hospital-based physicians doing this. Other examples include chiropractors who, after twenty-five years, are just done with doing adjustments and acupuncturists who embrace Chinese Medicine yet also want to appeal to a wider range of patients by using a more Western-oriented approach based on lab work.

I have a unique perspective, having seen so many transitioning practitioners go through the various predictable phases involved in this type of practice management makeover. Part of our training program includes strategy sessions on how to avoid the most common pitfalls and how to maximize your strengths to speed the difficult transition period along.

VETERANS

The third group I see wants to grow and scale their existing practice. They are experienced practitioners who have been in business for five to twenty-five years. They already understand and practice functional medicine but not in an entirely "functional" way. Perhaps there is too much confusion with patients or staff about the mission and focus of the practice, or there are just too many supplements and labs to choose from, and too many challenging patients.

Many times I find that these veterans are bored by their existing treatment methods and tired of their existing practice. They know they can offer better care to their patients and are looking for a fresh start and a better work–life balance. Their main issues are that they lack a simple business model, are doing too many labs and carrying too many supplements, and are overworking themselves. Often they have complex and chronically ill patients and are ultimately just burned out.

The veterans are always the same. They have been to too many seminars, have taken so many courses and read so many books, and have set up clinics that serve patients well but don't serve themselves. They are overburdened by the chronically ill and most challenging patients. While extremely bright, well studied, and devoted, they have dug a functional medicine hole for themselves. I know this type well; in fact, some of my best friends are in this category. I'm not joking here. The truth is, I was in this category myself and it took quite a few years to dig out of it.

However, I can now say my practice serves me and helps me lead a healthy, physically active, satisfying life full of what I want: exercise, good food, plenty of rest, and time off in beautiful locations. I have time for family and time for friends. These days I even have time to track cars, and every couple months I devote a day to simply driving really fast at a raceway. I want to practice well into my late eighties and figure I'm twenty-plus years into a fifty-year career. In order to be at my peak for my patients, I need to be fully present for myself and those closest to me.

Throughout my years of practice, I've been on all possible sides of these arrangements, starting as an associate, then having a solo practice, and then building and owning a large integrative health clinic. Each has its pros and cons. One of my goals working with doctors in our training programs is to coach people along the track that best suits them.

Within each of these scenarios are ideal ways to obtain maximum revenue. A solo practice with low overhead and exceptional marketing is one way. A group practice with joint ownership and a shared clear clinical model is another. Lastly, an associate relationship with a desirable cut of overall revenue can work in your favor, as an associate position leads to low stress and high financial returns even if you are giving 40 to 60 percent of your collections to a senior partner.

I want to share the clinical model and business model that has worked extremely well for me and for many of the practitioners who have taken courses at the Kalish Institute. Whether you're a newcomer, transitioning, or a veteran, I am confident we have something enriching to offer you.

4

WHAT IT TAKES TO GROW A PRACTICE

I talk to doctors by the hundreds every year and have watched several thousand practices grow and several thousand others fail. I can see what works and doesn't work, and I can see what we all as practitioners think we need to do versus what really needs to be done. In Burton White's book *Raising a Happy, Unspoiled Child*, White reveals over thirty years of social science research that showed the difference between what it really takes to raise a happy, unspoiled child versus what parents think it would take. Much of this is counterintuitive. What the authors did was study happy, unspoiled children and then, over decades of research, reverse engineer how they were raised to develop their theories. Using these theories, they successfully taught to parents how to achieve their parenting goals. It worked!

I've done the same thing with functional medicine practices. Having built several of my own and having watched my colleagues try to build their practices over twenty years ago, I've taken note of what's worked in the real world and what hasn't. I've imparted that knowledge to the hundreds of practitioners we've trained at the Kalish Institute, and guess what? It works! It's neither a mystery nor is it particularly complex. Just like parenting though, it becomes easy, almost predictable, to fall into certain traps and key phases, and our job at the Kalish Institute is to point out those problems ahead of time so you can cruise into a relatively pain-free growth period for your business.

WHAT DOCTORS SAY THEY NEED/WANT

What I hear from most from doctors is:

- ○ "I just need more new patients, and I'm not sure how to do the marketing for new patients well."

- ○ "Patients can't afford all this. I need a less expensive way to get started."

- ○ "In my area of X city in X state, there really isn't a market for this. I think I need to move somewhere else."

- ○ "I can't afford all the start-up costs associated with building a new practice model."

- ○ "I can't afford your class."

- ○ "Patients don't seem that interested in this, or they are a little interested or a lot interested only if their insurance will pay for it."

- ○ "I'd like to talk with you about my three most difficult cases that don't seem to be responding to any treatments anyone has ever used. Would this help them? Where would I start?"

- ○ "I have a very busy practice with chronically ill patients and I can't seem to get ahead financially. I'm busy—actually, I work most every day of the week—but I don't end up with much money at the end of the year."

- ○ "I'm tired of being a _____ (insurance-based MD, DC, ND, LAc, PT, NP, RN, etc.) and I still want to help patients, but

I can't work this many hours any longer and I want a better work–life balance."

○ "I have a great practice in functional medicine. I just need to get it organized and streamlined. There's so much information out there that I'm not sure where to start with every new patient."

○ "I'm comparing your program to other programs out there. How is yours different?"

○ "How much business advice is given in your class? I really want to focus on the business-building aspect of all this."

At the Kalish Institute, we see successful practices following the same model—mastery of a clinical system that is reproducible and will work for most of your patients (with the occasional exception, of course) combined with a business model that addresses your infrastructure needs to make it all profitable. I'd like to explain the clinical and business models to show you how they integrate seamlessly.

By way of an example, let's look at the three P's in regards to building an integrated business/clinical model. You can view this single project from three different angles: the practitioner's view, the patient's view, and the view from the business side of the practice. To begin, let's look at the first five steps that you, your patients, and your staff will follow to get a sense of what "integrating" a clinical model with a business model means. Think of it like buying a franchise, such as if you were going to set up a McDonalds. You would have employees, customers, and the product. The employees would have clear steps to follow, your customers would need to learn certain things so they could purchase what they want, and your place of business would need to have cash registers, a deep fryer, and so on.

THE FIRST FIVE STEPS

Practitioner's Viewpoint

Step 1: A new-patient session that shows the patient how his or her chief complaints are directly related to the three body systems: hormones (adrenals), GI, and detox.

Step 2: Get the patient enrolled in lifestyle changes.

Step 3: Labs are back. Discuss findings on lab work and motivation for starting the patient's individualized six-month supplement program.

Step 4: Follow up with labs and supplements.

Step 5: With chief complaints resolved, move to long-term maintenance programs to prevent chief complaints from returning.

Patient's Viewpoint

Step 1: Learn how my chief complaints are coming from a breakdown in my body systems and how there are lab tests to detect the problems I have (shifting away fom symptom-oriented thinking).

Step 2: Learn how to implement all four lifestyle changes for diet, exercise, sleep, and meditation.

Step 3: See how the labs exactly correspond to my problems and how they reveal the underlying causes of my symptoms.

Step 4: Begin the long haul of fixing the issues we've found.

Step 5: Learn how to maintain my newfound health and vitality with ongoing lifestyle changes and a maintenance supplement program.

Practice-Building Viewpoint

Step 1: Determine the new-patient intake process, the logistics of distributing labs, billing, and new-patient questionnaires, and start bonding with staff.

Step 2: Determine what happens to the patient after the first visit. Follow up to be sure labs are completed and to get the lifestyle coaching started. The key element here is to use the time when you're waiting for the labs to come back to get the diet, exercise, meditation, and sleep patterns improved. Most patients will experience significant improvements simply by eliminating gluten, dairy, soy, caffeine, alcohol, and sugar from their diet, but getting them to do this is the first big challenge for this step.

Step 3: When labs are back, the patient needs to be contacted and scheduled for another appointment. After the lab presentation of findings session, put the patient on a supplement program. The logistical issues here abound! Many practitioners I've worked with do a great job up to this point and then everything falls apart. Some patients buy a month's worth of supplements and then you never hear from them again. Other patients don't buy supplements from you at all and try to figure out how to get them cheaply online. This moment requires business systems and follow up. Your office can sell three- or six-month programs at one time. Get patient follow-up visits scheduled and be sure to e-mail and call to verify that the patient will come to the appointments. The best thing we can do is follow up, follow up, follow up.

Step 4: Long-term follow-up mostly depends on your staff. E-mail reminders to patients along with a monthly newsletter to serve as a general reminder of your existence make a difference. I use a preset questionnaire that allows one of my staff to make calls and get caught up with patient progress between office visits with me.

Step 5: This last step is the key to your long-term financial success. Once patients are better, they will drop out and stop buying labs and supplements from you. That naturally occurs. To create a long-term passive revenue model and, more importantly, for the long-term health of your patients and to prevent people from slipping back to whatever state of poor health brought them in, you can set up long-term maintenance programs with a yearly check-in and a regular auto-ship of a three-month supply of supplements. I believe we all need to check in with a professional to stay healthy these days. Life happens (sick kids or sick parents, a divorce or a surgery, etc.), but these obstacles throw patients back to their prior poor health. Long-term maintenance provides a way for you to periodically check in with people and help them before life events build up so much that they start to suffer physical consequences.

Simply put, the model starts and ends like this: First assess and correct the chief complaints, then fix the underlying root causes and change lifestyle factors, and finally follow up and move to long-term maintenance. If you solve significant health problems at the outset, it's logical that you and the patient will want to keep the process going. Patient left on their own will slip back. The diet fails, sugar and caffeine creep back, there's not enough time for meditation, and gradually their health falls apart again. In addition to correcting the initial complaints, the long-term health of these people also matters. In ancient China, doctors were paid by healthy people who would STOP paying their physicians when they became sick!

As you integrate your clinical model and business model and develop all the required nuances, your practice will grow and increase in profitability. Two nice side effects of the maintenance programs include an ongoing revenue stream for you as well as the ongoing health benefits for the patient. Just think about the clinical/business model dentists have developed. While the dentist sees patients when they have tooth pain, at the same time the recurring revenue of twice-yearly cleanings brings in consistent income and offers the consumer maintenance that helps prevent major problems from developing in the first place.

In our example, having 100 patients buying an $80-per-month supplement program with a multivitamins, EFAs, minerals, antioxidants, and probiotics adds up to $8,000 in monthly revenue. That's $96,000 a year, leaving you (assuming a 50 percent margin) with $48,000 of profit. This model allows you relief from the constant financial pressures of driving in new patients and makes you more able to focus on what we all signed up for—healing. It allows us as health professionals to change people's lives, reduce human suffering, and improve human potential.

5

SETTING YOURSELF UP
FOR SUCCESS

THE ALL-CASH BUSINESS MODEL

Cash practices get better patient compliance and better patient outcomes because the patient invests his or her hard-earned money and in doing so takes personal responsibility for the outcomes. In our culture, when we put our own money down, we care. When we put our own money down, we value the object of concern. When we put our own money down, we take things seriously and want to get our value. It's nice when someone else offers to pay for something or when we pay for things indirectly, but that financial disconnect weakens our attention and focus.

For example, we all pay, indirectly, for the roads we drive on (through taxes), but do you take a strong interest in local road quality or do anything to maintain them? Probably not. Now consider the walkway to your house, which you own. That responsibility and ownership makes a difference. If a step on your front porch gets damaged, you'd probably fix it quickly. The same applies with healthcare. When patients spend their own dollars, they care.

The results you get in your functional medicine practice depend 80 percent on adherence to lifestyle changes and 20 percent on supplement programs or medications. So we need completely buy into the lifestyle changes, and we can achieve that with cash-paying patients. The fact that they've spent their own money on a program creates incentive for them to take the lifestyle changes seriously. That ends up getting you the results you want—and it changes lives.

Cash is also convenient for you as a business owner since you eliminate all accounts receivable issues and collect 100 percent of what you are owed on the day you do the work. No insurance forms, no waiting for reimbursements, and no reductions in your fees. Ever. Ultimately, the all-cash model gets better results and faster results, which in turn will help you build a referral-based business.

PATIENT COMMUNICATION SKILLS

I was born in 1964 and grew up in Berkeley, California, in the 1970s. Free speech, free love, and the Grateful Dead were in full bloom. Did I learn one thing about how to communicate with other people? Nope. I entered my initial years as a clinician with zero patient communication skills. I was so naïve that I thought patients cared about what I cared about. It's embarrassing to look back on it now, but during my first years of functional medicine, I would take the time to explain cytochrome P-450 enzymes systems to patients! I loved the biochemistry and honestly didn't know what I was supposed to be discussing anyway. I knew I was supposed to do thirty-minute consults, so I filled the time with what was of interest to me.

Fortunately, one of my mentors, Dr. Glenn Frieder, saw my dysfunction and starting dragging me to communication workshops—one class after another—and finally I learned. I was supposed to be dealing with the patient's concerns, interests, and issues, not talking about mine. This led me, over the course of several years, to develop highly effective patient communication techniques specific to functional medicine. I've developed many of these, but the basic technique to start with is what I call the "condition/description technique." The patient has a "condition" and you need to provide a "description" of why that condition will be perfectly addressed with a functional medicine approach.

PICK A NICHE

Does the place where you get your hair cut also sell fruit? Does your dry cleaner offer to clean windows? Of course not. Every business has a niche. Some businesses just do hair, that's it. Maybe they sell hair care products and do waxing and nails too, but it's all about body aesthetics. Some businesses just clean clothing, and they do that one thing well. You go there, utilize their service, and no one questions the rationale of how that business is structured.

In conventional medicine, there are many specialties, and each one provides a limited repertoire of services. For some reason, in natural medicine many practitioners feel they need to be all things to all people. I know I did. I figured I could work with kids, adults, and seniors; men and women; the pregnant; the depressed; the autoimmune cases; and those recovering from cancer. The idea of turning someone away or focusing on one area was never presented to me as an option.

So here I go with my advice: You can choose your practice. You can work with whatever group of people you want to. Just figure out what floats your boat. Do you want to work with pregnant women, or maybe women who can't get pregnant? Pediatrics or geriatrics? Those recovering from cancer treatment, or professional athletes? With endless choices, you can pick what's most engaging for you and pursue that group.

You can also have a general practice. Many of us, myself included, do. But over all these years I've always had a niche: female hormone balancing. So I work with men and women, kids and older adults, but have always focused on what I call the "Big Five": fat, fatigue, depression, GI problems, and female hormones.

Having a niche allows you to focus your marketing efforts, and it makes it much easier to explain what you do to prospective new patients. It helps people understand what you're about and makes it easier for them to decide to choose you and refer others to your practice.

START WITH EASY PATIENTS

The Kalish Institute attracts exclusively top-level practitioners. The best healers tend to attract the most challenging patients to treat, and for all of you with over five years in practice, you know exactly what I mean. One day you realize you've fixed one complicated case, only to have five other even more complicated patients referred in. Eventually you end up with a chronic-illness-based practice. Some of you will love this and want to run a chronic illness practice for your entire career. This I commend, as you are extraordinary and special. All my teachers were just like you; they all had chronic illness practices, working with the sickest people in their community and making a lifetime career by impacting this patient population. It's rewarding and satisfying work. You all make a huge difference.

What I learned about myself was surprising. I didn't like having a chronic illness practice. I was an early star, having trained with the best within my first five years of practice. My clinical nutrition skills were extraordinary, and I quickly attracted a chronic illness patient base. I had patients flying in from Europe and driving down from LA. It was a rush and a thrill to have that kind of attention and to feel that I could really make a difference for these people.

But after about four years in that first practice, I crashed. I was burned out, despondent, and not enjoying the work as I had in the past. Then my son was born and I instantly realized two things: one, I wanted to have a lot more free time to spend with him and didn't want to work the hours required to run a chronic illness practice where each patient takes extra time and care; and two, I wanted to earn more money so we could buy a house and start a college fund.

I realized I had to look at my calling, my journey as a healer, and my practice as a business endeavor. For the first time in my life, I focused on the money. I needed to start attracting an easier patient base, and to do this I started lecturing throughout my community on female hormone balancing. This worked, and within a year I had a steady stream of peri-menopausal women coming in, which created the foundation of my practice for years.

Those of you in practice for a long time (I know you're excellent healers or you wouldn't have read this far) may have found yourself in a similar situation. This is also something to consider for those of you just starting a functional medicine practice. Ultimately, where do you want your practice to end up?

For everyone learning functional medicine, new and transitioning practitioners all, it's imperative to learn on easy cases. Whenever you are at a seminar, the first thing you do when you learn something new is think of what patients you can apply the knowledge to. Oftentimes it's the most difficult patient cases—or those we couldn't completely solve—that compel our continued learning. So it's natural that we would want to apply newfound principles to the hardest cases. There are several problems with this approach.

The first problem is that your success rate in applying any protocol to a challenging case will be low. The patients may respond or they may not, or they may take an extremely long time to respond. In any case, you'll get disillusioned and start to think what you're learning doesn't work very well. The second problem is that you won't know enough in the very beginning to problem solve these challenging cases, so you'll be more likely than not to make mistakes when learning on the most difficult patients. I have seen many practitioners, excited about functional medicine, end up stymied in this way. Their results aren't consistent, they make mistakes, their patients get worse, and they soon drop out of the functional medicine field.

I don't want that to happen. I want you to be successful. So start with easy cases. You'll get more consistent results; maybe eight out of ten patients will get better instead of two out of ten. You'll make less consequential mistakes, and learning will not be as painful. You'll get enthusiasm, and you'll get referrals. Then as you build up your confidence, after you develop your clinical skills and business model, then you can start to expand out to treating the difficult cases.

CHAPTER

6

CHOOSING A TRAINING PROGRAM

You may be wondering how to get your functional medicine practice started. It's confusing. There is no single clear path to establishing yourself. It could take you several years of trial and error to find the right path, and accessing objective information on the next best steps can be difficult. Most people promoting themselves have an agenda—the obvious one, money. Lab companies, supplement companies, and private training programs all are looking to increase their client base. Quite honestly, I am too. However, I have a unique niche. I am interested in finding the right people for my program. If you're not the right person, I will tell you. Why would I turn away business? First of all, there are more practitioners that need training than we have the capacity to handle. The Kalish Institute utilizes small groups limited to twenty-five students per class and one teacher (me). This restricts our capacity.

Additionally, I have found over years of practice that my integrity is of utmost importance and that if I give a doctor the best advice, which may be to do a different program than mine, that it always benefits me later. That doctor may sign up for our classes in a few years or refer a friend. That's just how the world of integrative medicine works. It's a small world, and my integrity is my main focus.

Why would I suggest you do a different program? If you can't really afford our fees, you should be starting with a less expensive class so you can get started without taking on debt that you will regret later. If you need more intellectual- or research-based coursework, we don't provide that at all, but several other courses do. If you want to learn how to read blood work, we don't teach that but other programs do an excellent job of it. If you want to learn all about diabetes or cardiovascular treatments, again we are limited and don't offer coursework in those areas but other programs do. So let's take a moment and review the types of courses available and what they offer.

PROGRAMS AVAILABLE

To get you familiarized with the names of the major courses available, there are the Institute of Functional Medicine and their broad offering of in-person seminars and certifications; the Academy of Anti-Aging Medicine, known as A4M; Functional Medicine University, a 100 percent online course; and Functional Diagnostic Nutrition. Then there are individual practitioners like myself who offer courses. You may have specific needs in terms of gaps in your training that need to be filled, or you may be starting out fresh and unsure of the first logical step. Additionally, supplement companies like Designs for Health, Orthomolecular, and Apex offer many weekend courses and webinars highlighting various clinical topics.

Institute of Functional Medicine (IFM)

The Institute of Function Medicine started it all. I was at Dr. Jeffrey Bland's seminars year after year in the 1990s, excited to be learning about this emerging field. Now with many decades of experience, IFM has well-established courses that form the backbone of professional training in functional medicine. They have a modular training program where you attend various modules in different cities, which leads to certification. They tend to have the brightest and best teachers in the field, many of whom are founders of functional medicine and have been working in this specialty for decades. Their curriculum is modeled more like a traditional medical school, with an emphasis on research and a focus on patient-centered care and embracing both the latest science in the field as well as lifestyle issues like meditation and diet.

Everyone should complete IFM courses, at least those that are of special interest, if not the entire certification program. I'm personally not certified since certification wasn't available when I was attending their seminars, but I attended everything they offered year after year as I was being trained in the early and mid-1990s.

Academy of Anti-Aging Medicine (A4M)

A4M has a top-notch reputation. They started off with a focus on anti-aging medicine but now strongly incorporate functional medicine into their programs. I've not personally attended their workshops, but most of the MDs I work closely with have and rave about them. Because of the original focus on anti-aging medicine and the use of prescription hormones, I would think this group is more MD centric and has fewer acupuncturists, chiropractors, and naturopaths involved, which has its advantages and disadvantages depending on your background. I have interacted with several of A4M's faculty and certainly feel they are inclusive and open to all professionals joining their educational events.

Functional Medicine University (FMU)

Functional Medicine University is an online program. FMU gives a preset curriculum delivered in an organized way, and all the doctors I've spoken to who have taken the course have had positive things to say about it. FMU does not have a clinical application component or a business development component, being more focused on general education in the diverse areas within functional medicine.

Functional Diagnostic Nutrition (FDN)

Functional Diagnostic Nutrition is also an online program. FDN offers training mostly to non-licensed practitioners such as personal trainers and nutritionists and has a strong clinical application component with a large emphasis on nutrition. Again, I've spoken with dozens of their graduates and they have generally good things to say about their experience.

FM Town/Dr. Dicken Weatherby

For those of you looking to learn how to perform functional assessments of blood chemistries, my good friend and long-term collaborator Dr. Dicken Weatherby has a blood chemistry course that is highly regarded (it is available through his company, FM Town). Dr. Weatherby has been teaching blood chemistry for decades, and many of my students go on to do his coursework and many of his students interested in the testing I cover come over to our program.

In the next chapter, we'll talk about the Kalish Institute and what it offers. Bottom line, your decision about which program to choose should all come down to what's best for you.

7

THE KALISH TRAINING PROGRAM AND COMMUNITY

In 1997, after four years of seeing patients and two years of intensive studies in functional medicine and clinical nutrition, I began to develop training materials with Dr. Bill Timmins. In essence I became his sounding board, #1 student, junior doctor, and transcriber. We had a father/son, teacher/disciple relationship, and I was eager to soak up his clinical knowledge and put it on paper. I began writing patient education guides and became his assistant teacher at the functional medicine seminars he produced.

Nine years later, in late 2006, I began my own functional medicine training program based on my interpretation of his work. Back in 1986, while in my early twenties, I'd become fascinated with technology and the early personal computers that IBM was producing. With the help of friends who were computer engineers, I built custom machines and started a computer consulting business, specializing in systems for law firms. Naturally, when I began my own functional medicine training program, I wanted to use the latest technology and deliver the materials online in a webinar format.

Now, in 2015, the Kalish Institute is at the forefront of Internet-based learning and has some of the most sophisticated software in the industry. Living next door to Silicon Valley has its perks. What excites me the most about our advanced technology is the user experience and the concept of community building and online interactive learning.

The Kalish Institute offers a specific niche within the larger framework of functional medicine education, with a specific clinical model and business model for starting a practice. It's a practical course, 100 percent oriented toward business development and mastering basic clinical skills in three areas: neuroendocrine, GI, and detoxification. We teach doctors how to create a business around functional medicine principles, using simple lab tests for adrenals, female hormones, GI function, detoxification, the brain, and nutrient replacement.

Our initial six-month course presents all the business fundamentals. We start by covering new-patient interview skills and provide new-patient questionnaires. We go over lab presentation and report-of-finding skills and then get into specific supplement protocols based on lab results. We look at which labs to start with and what sequence to put your protocols together. We address even what seem like simple issues, like how many supplements a given patient can handle at one time and, if you're limited by how many supplements to use, which are the most crucial. We discuss how to take a complex series of lab findings and reduce all the information to a program the patient will actually be compliant with. It's practical, accessible information for people at the stage of practice building.

Then we address business development skills and the clinical skills around the fundamentals. In Level One, we spend six months covering business skills and practice management issues and at the same time look at clinical aspects such as adrenals, female hormones, and GI workups. In Level Two (the advanced course), we look in depth at organic acids testing and delve into treatments for the brain and detoxification programs. This advanced coursework also looks at methylation, mitochondrial function, and the role of antioxidants, amino acids, and B vitamins. It's a more complex area that we then link back to the basic model of three body systems: neuroendocrine, GI, and detox.

When you join the Kalish Institute, you have access to your course materials, including all the pre-recorded lectures and course materials. At the same time, you gain access to the community feature, which is like a functional medicine Facebook. This aspect of the program has three sections: community, classes, and content. In the community section, you post a personal profile for other practitioners to see, then you can look up other students based on common interests, professional affiliation, or location. So you could find all the other acupuncturists in the program or locate other MDs in the part of Canada where you live.

Most practitioners who start at the Kalish Institute have had previous training in functional medicine and are excited to learn the business fundamentals and simple clinical protocols used to get a new practice off the ground or to streamline an existing practice. We also work with people who are brand new to functional medicine and are ready for a business model now. If you want more of the theory and research behind functional medicine, if you'd rather complete your training in person versus online and on the phone, or if you want a specific module like cardio-metabolic or something less expensive, then the other programs I mentioned may be better options.

As I travel around the country visiting practices of our graduates, the impact the Kalish Method has had is remarkable. We have just the right tools to propel practitioners to the next level.

8

THE KALISH METHOD'S FIVE PILLARS OF BUILDING A PRACTICE

The Kalish Method uses five pillars that have proven to build a successful functional medicine practice. To give you an even better idea of whether the Kalish Institute courses would benefit you, let's look at those pillars now.

PILLAR #1: CHOOSE THE RIGHT PATIENTS

The best way to start your practice is by focusing on the Big Five:

- ○ Weight Gain

- ○ Fatigue

- ○ Depression

- ○ GI problems

- ○ Female hormone imbalances

Now, you may be asking yourself why these five?

These five issues are, first, amenable to correction through basic functional medicine protocols, and, second, very common in the general population as well as in existing patient populations in chiropractic offices. So, focusing on the Big Five is the simple key that unlocked my practice success and is the very first principle in the Kalish Method.

Later, if you want to make your life more complicated, you can expand to more complex cases.

PILLAR #2: FOCUS ON THE THREE BODY SYSTEMS

It's easy. Focus on three labs and three body systems.

The three body systems are those taught to me by Dr. Timmins in his idea of "Treatment Flow":

Hormones, then GI, then detoxification.

Now, you may be wondering why I focus on just three when other training programs focus on a matrix of eight or a functional hierarchy of twelve organ systems. The reason is clear. I like to keep it simple. Imbalances in the three body systems are responsible for almost every health problem and are at the core of the Big Five. Rather than me just talking about this, let me show you how it works in our patients.

Most health problems start when we are under stress (adrenals), which leads to digestive problems. After a while, the chronic digestive problems (GI) create an accumulation of toxins in the system leading to problems with liver function (detoxification).

One of the first questions I always get when I explain this is, "In what order do I work with these systems?"

Here's my simple answer:

We work these problems in the order they originally occur: first correct the adrenal (or hormone) imbalances, then address the GI system, and then look at detoxification.

Another question I often get is, "How do these organ systems relate to one another?" Let's take a look:

Each body system relies on the other for its normal function, but most health problems start in body system #1, the hormonal system (primarily in the adrenal hormone system, because when we are under stress, stress hormones increase). This rise in adrenal stress hormones is usually precipitated by a major life event such as a death in the family, divorce, childbirth, or just plain old overworking. Sound familiar? If we are under prolonged or chronic stress, then the three body systems break down in a predictable manner:

1. The stress causes adrenal exhaustion.

2. After several years of adrenal exhaustion, the second body system, GI, falters and we develop GI infections or food reactions or what's called "leaky gut," because the adrenals regulate GI immune cells.

3. If leaky gut goes on for years, then all the toxins from the GI tract are dumped on the liver and we end up with liver detoxification issues.

Contrast this predictable pattern with how the systems evolved to function.

As you can see, all three body systems central to the Kalish Method are in homeostatic balance, and that's what we are aiming for when restoring optimal function.

Now, let's bring this back to the Kalish Method. When the majority of your patients suffer from the Big Five complaints, you will have many advantages. First, you will master the various protocols, working on your patient scripts, honing your skills on writing protocols, and having an efficient inventory system so you are using the same products over and over. Plus, not only are these Big Five all problems that lend themselves to correction with functional medicine; they are also not easy for conventional medicine to treat successfully, so you will have a high rate of success and be able to work with patients that fall between the cracks of the conventional medical system. This will lead to more and more referrals from people with Big Five complaints, and more and more repetition and practice will make you better and better quickly.

Imagine that, as a chiropractor, you had every new patient for a year complain about something completely different—toe pain, ankle pain, knee pain, hip pain, eyelid pain, ear pain, hair follicle pain, etc. You'd go crazy trying to treat all these problems and conditions, and most of them, like hair follicle pain, you probably couldn't help even if you were the best chiropractor in the world.

But with my model of functional medicine using the Kalish Method, we focus on the basics as I do in my chiropractic practice: headaches, neck pain, back pain, and some extremity issues, over and over. I know I can help most of these patients, and I know that my solutions are far safer and usually more effective than the conventional medical approach of muscle relaxants and pain medication. My functional medicine model is one born of a chiropractic mind-set to "treat the cause, not the symptom" and "let's resolve these issues without resorting to dangerous drugs or surgeries."

PILLAR #3: SPEAK THE PATIENT'S LANGUAGE

We must learn to translate the patient's language of symptoms into the functional medicine language of body systems using what I call condition/description technique.

Patients will gladly rush to pay for your services when you correctly translate the language of their symptoms.

Patients want to know they can get better. They need hope (from your confidence in your techniques), they need to understand how you can help them, and they need to feel that your functional medicine model was designed for people exactly like them.

We can provide this by translating their language (the language of symptoms and complaints) into the Kalish Method Clinical Model language of (1) underlying causes leading to (2) problems with the three body systems and (3) this ultimately resulting in their symptoms. It's exactly the same model as: (1) a subluxation leading to (2) a problem with joint mobility, muscle tension, and pressure on nerves, which (3) ultimately leads to pain (symptom).

Given that, how do we get patients to buy that first test?

Easy.

Attach the need for that test to an obvious system.

In the Kalish Method, we work with three body systems in the order of hormones (primarily adrenal hormones), GI, and then detox. So the very first test your patients will need is an adrenal stress test.

The key to having every patient walk out of your clinic with an adrenal stress test is linking the symptoms they are experiencing to adrenal exhaustion. This takes some practice and studying of scripts. The good news is I've formulated every script you can imagine and you just need to memorize them, not create them from scratch.

To get started, you only need to learn scripts for the Big Five, which you can do at one a day in about a week. First, you need to understand how adrenal exhaustion is at the root of fat, fatigue, depression, GI problems, and female hormones issues. Once you understand this, it's easy to explain to patients why the test is important and how, when done right, this will result in a near 100 percent patient compliance.

Let's look at some real-life examples.

Case #1. We have a patient, Susan, complaining of fatigue and weight gain. Sounds familiar. It should, because that describes a couple hundred million Americans today.

You would say, "Well, Susan, I noticed that besides the neck pain that's been bothering you since the accident, you also listed fatigue and weight gain as primary complaints. It's interesting, because fatigue and weight gain are really two aspects of one central underlying problem. Have you heard of the adrenal glands before, or the hormone cortisol? When we're under stress, we produce large amounts of the stress hormone cortisol, and this, over time, can burn out the adrenal glands and lead to what we call adrenal exhaustion, or adrenal burnout. Once our adrenals get burned out from stress—and there are three major sources of stress: emotional, dietary, and pain and inflammatory stress—cortisol becomes depleted and we get physically exhausted and are tired all the time, especially in the late afternoon."

You would continue with, "If the adrenal burnout goes on for long enough, then cortisol's role in regulating our fat-burning metabolism starts to fail and we store body fat, especially around the abdomen. This is really the body's attempt to protect us, since for most of human history high stress has been linked with lack of food, such as from a famine or a war. We adapt to survive during periods of high stress by storing or saving body fat. But as the adrenals burn out, we damage our metabolism, and even when the stress is over, the metabolism stays in this state of disarray, unable to burn fat even when we eat well and exercise."

Finish with, "If we can test and correct your cortisol, we can get your energy levels back up to normal, where they were before you _____ (had kids, went to law school, got divorced, etc.), and if we can test and correct your cortisol levels, we can repair your damaged metabolism and get your fat-burning system up and running again. It's a pretty simple test, costs a little over a hundred dollars, and from the lab results I can design a nutritional program along with lifestyle changes so you can heal your adrenal glands and get your energy back and lose weight."

Who could say no to that?

Case #2. Your patient, Jim, is complaining of back pain, depression, and IBS.

You would say, "Okay, Jim, I know you listed depression and IBS as chief complaints right after your back pain, so I'd like to talk about some natural solutions that could really make a difference. You know when we're under stress, there is this stress hormone called cortisol that gets depleted.

The more stress we are under, the more depleted our cortisol gets, and eventually we can end up in what's called adrenal burnout, or adrenal exhaustion. If your adrenals burn out severely, then depression sets in since your body doesn't have enough of the right hormones to keep your brain feeling good."

Continue with, "We can test and correct adrenal exhaustion and rebuild this system so your mood and energy levels will improve. It's not that complicated because the programs are all designed based on a saliva test. A lot of times we see adrenal exhaustion along with a digestive problem like heartburn or IBS, and the more exhausted your adrenals become, the more digestive issues tend to pop up. This happens because cortisol, the main adrenal hormone, regulates the immune cells in the lining of the digestive tract, and, as the adrenal hormones fail, we get more and more immune cell compromise in the gut, causing what we call leaky gut. When the gut becomes leaky, it means the lining of the digestive tract isn't working properly and substances leak into our system, creating even more digestive distress and depression-type issues. In fact, there's a large body of research now that looks specifically at brain/gut connections. Most people have heard of this in regards to ulcers. We all know that when people are really stressed out, ulcers tend to flare up. This is a classic example of a brain/gut connection."

Finish with, "If we can get your adrenals tested and measure your cortisol, I can set up a supplement program to help improve your mood and reduce the depression, and at the same time we can get into diet changes like giving up gluten and keeping your blood sugar stable, which will improve adrenal and gut health. Most people notice a significant improvement in the first three to four weeks of a program. The programs don't last forever, and once we test and correct your adrenal glands, you can get off the supplements and maintain your improvement with lifestyle changes alone. Why don't we get started by testing your cortisol, and next week you can come back in and we can get you set on the diet changes that will really make a difference."

Really, it all comes down to speaking the patient's language. If you explain to your patients what's going on in their body and how it can be fixed— using words they understand—they'll respond favorably. Success then follows.

PILLAR #4: START WITH THE RIGHT LAB TESTS

Every patient can be started with the same lab tests; you don't need to reinvent the wheel every time. We test the hormones, GI tract, and detoxification systems in that order with every patient presenting with the Big Five.

Treatment Approach:

- Start a gluten-free diet.
- Test the cortisol and DHEA levels, and treat any abnormalities.
- Test and treat any digestive infections.
- Retest the hormone levels.
- Retest the gut.

Treating Complicated Cases

In complicated cases, the order that we address the three body systems varies slightly. In these patients, we address the adrenal primary, GI primary, and detox primary systems.

Adrenal Primary: This is the fastest route to get through programs for the average patient. It potentially uses the fewest number of supplements at any one time since the programs are sequential one after the other and the only overlap would be adrenals plus GI and adrenals plus detox. Focus on getting the patient feeling better though lifestyle changes and improving adrenal function prior to initiating potentially stressful treatments. Spend the first two months doing adrenal-only protocols with diet to reduce GI inflammation and prepare for GI programs. Use diet and lifestyle to promote detoxification (such as hydration and eating fiber-rich, nutrient-dense foods so antioxidants and fiber increase removal of toxins). The adrenals control SIgA and regulate detox enzymes, so improving adrenal function improves gut immunity and detox capacity.

GI Primary: This is for people with more extensive GI inflammation where diet and adrenals alone are not enough to prepare for the GI killing phase. Focus on leaky gut repair protocols throughout the entire six months, including from the very beginning of the program and in some cases prior to adrenal labs coming back. Once the adrenal program and lifestyle changes kick in along with the gut repair, then go to GI killing phase with more confidence that it will be effective.

Detox Primary A, B, C, and D: This is for highly toxic patients who will react poorly to GI killing since it creates toxins and significantly increases oxidative stress, placing a large burden on the liver. Therefore, starting to improve detox capacity first is key to avoiding side effects of the GI programs. Then, as the GI killing starts, the liver support continues to be important so the patient can handle the burden coming from GI tract and being dumped on liver. Extra highly toxic patients won't even be able to handle the adrenal products and will need to go it alone with the detox programs first, working their way up to being able to tolerate the adrenal programs. With patients that are this toxic, you may also want to use a second variation where the adrenals come last.

PILLAR #5: LOW OVERHEAD AND USE OF TECHNOLOGY

Focus on low overhead and use technology as much as possible to facilitate patient services and patient education. This includes:

○ Business fundamentals

○ Lab Tests

○ Scripts

○ Protocols

○ Supplement Inventory

○ Human resources and setup

And my last success tip for you:

As soon as you start to get a little bit busy, **set up the best business systems possible:**

○ Use online scheduling with auto-reminder e-mails.

○ Get clear about how much you will charge for your functional medicine services.

○ Never discount supplements; the retail prices are fair as they are.

○ Leverage technology as much as you can:

- Type up all patient programs on a computer so they are legible and easy for the staff to understand.

- Website (Wordpress)

- Online scheduler (Appointment Plus)

- Autoresponders

- Quickbooks

- Folder hierarchy

- Forms

- Electronic backup system (Raid Array)

○ Once you had functional medicine services to a clinic, use patient management software for reminder systems, sending and receiving e-mails, posting lab results, and all the other issues that come up.

○ Have a business coach in your life. I have had many business coaches over the years, and they have taught me most of what I know.

○ Attend business seminars at least once a year, if not more regularly.

SOME FINAL WORDS

In the past nine years, many doctors have passed through the Kalish Institute and just under one thousand practitioners have taken our courses. The interest in functional medicine spans the full range of our field, from naturopaths and chiropractors to medical doctors, nurse practitioners, pharmacists, and physical therapists. We have conducted special trainings specifically for acupuncturists, nutritionists, addiction counselors, and therapists. This work applies in many contexts, whether you treat musculoskeletal conditions and want to add a functional medicine component, if you're a therapist who knows the body–mind connection runs deep, or if you're a medical doctor who wants to expand beyond the prescribing of medications to a more holistic framework.

Of all the people we have attracted to the training program over the years, notably among them were two physicians from the Mayo Clinic—Brent Bauer, MD, Director of Mayo Clinic's Integrative Medicine Department in Rochester, Minnesota, and Larry Bergstrom, MD, Director of Mayo Clinic's Integrative Medicine Department on their Arizona campus. After six months of classes, I flew to Minnesota and then Arizona to meet with Drs. Bauer and Bergstrom in person. Later I came up with a research proposal to look at the efficacy of the adrenal and GI protocols taught at the Kalish

Institute. In the fall of 2014, we launched a six-month research study on the Kalish Method with Dr. Bauer and Sue Cutshall, a clinical nurse specialist at Mayo Clinic. Our data collection is now completed and the study will be published later this year.

This assures me that functional medicine's time has come. We can now start showing evidence of the effectiveness of these longstanding protocols handed down to me from my teachers. We've reached the tipping point, and it's now time for functional medicine to gradually move into mainstream acceptance as a viable option for addressing the current health problems we face. I can't imagine a better moment for a student to come and be trained, to learn the basics of functional medicine, and to start a practice in this most-rewarding field.

The Kalish Institute dedicates itself to providing the educational opportunities required to make a real difference in patients' lives and get your functional medicine business up and running. For more information, visit www.kalishinstitute.com.

Made in the USA
San Bernardino, CA
25 February 2016